All About Land Hermit Crabs

by Mervin F. Roberts

A BOOK FOR BEGINNERS, FULLY ILLUSTRATED
WITH MAGNIFICENT FULL COLOR PHOTOGRAPHS

The author wishes to express his gratitude to
Thomas Arthur Cuccurullo, the youngster who
posed for the photos and who owns the hermit
crabs, and to Dr. Herbert R. Axelrod, who took the
photos.
Thanks also are due Pets Ahoy Pet Shop in Avon,
New Jersey for providing materials shown in
photographs in the book.

0-87666-920-8

Distributed in the U.S.A. by T.F.H. Publications, Inc., 211 West Sylvania Avenue, P.O. Box 27, Neptune City, N.J. 07753; in England by T.F.H. (Gt. Britain) Ltd., 13 Nutley Lane, Reigate, Surrey; in Canada to the book store and library trade by Clarke, Irwin & Company, Clarwin House, 791 St. Clair Avenue West, Toronto 10, Ontario; in Canada to the pet trade by Rolf C. Hagen Ltd., 3225 Sartelon Street, Montreal 382, Quebec; in Southeast Asia by Y.W. Ong, 9 Lorong 36 Geylang, Singapore 14; in Australia and the south Pacific by Pet Imports Pty. Ltd., P.O. Box 149, Brookvale 2100, N.S.W., Australia. Published by T.F.H. Publications Inc. Ltd., The British Crown Colony of Hong Kong.

Contents

Dried out cactus is ideal for hermit crabs, since it allows them to climb all over it . . . and hide inside it . . . yet still be seen. Photo by Dr. Herbert R. Axelrod.

This poor hermit crab has just outgrown his shell! He can't fit back in and might fall prey to parasites or dry out. Photo by Dr. Herbert R. Axelrod.

Foreword

All the mistakes are mine, this goes without saying; but what I must say is that were it not for Dr. Herbert R. Axelrod, A.A. Pare, Martin Wartman, Mrs. Clarita Haast, Dr. P. A. McLaughlin, the patient librarians at Kline Library—Yale University, and Edith R. Ritz, this little book would still be all talk.

Old Lyme, Connecticut
July, 1978

Introducing Your
Land Hermit Crab

So often among animals the names are deceptive or changed or wrong. For example, *chameleon* is derived from the French, which when translated to English reads "dwarf lion." Terrapins and tortoises are all really just turtles, and the Biblical reference to "the voice of the turtle—heard throughout the land" in the Song of Solomon is clearly the voice of the cooing pigeon sometimes called the "turtle dove." The Tasmanian wolf is not a dog-like wolf but is a marsupial more closely related to the kangaroo, and the sea lion is not a lion. The great classifier and namer of names (you know him as Carolus Linnaeus [1707-1788] the Swedish botanist) was known as Carl von Linne for the last 17 years of his life. These little inconsistencies set the stage for the subject of this book, the tree hermit crab also known as the land hermit crab, also known as the purple clawed hermit crab also known as the soldier crab.

It is certainly not arboreal, although some individuals do climb trees; in fact, it is not even totally terrestrial since it is water-borne for at least four stages of its early metamorphic life. Worse yet, I have watched these creatures and studied the literature and have yet to find a satisfactory reason for calling them "hermits." Actually, they seem to be gregarious.

Well, no matter. You now own or are about to own one (or a few) of these interesting, hardy, long lived, inexpensive, odorless, relatively quiet pets commonly known as land or tree hermit crabs.

7

One of the colorful marine hermit crabs, *Dardanus cenmanus*. For more information on marine hermit crabs see *Marine Hermit Crabs*, published by T.F.H. Publications. Photo by Scott Johnson.

What, scientifically speaking, do you have? Let's start at the top and work our way out to a branch and a few twigs in the Tree of Life, but please don't let minor contradictions upset you—remember von Linne-Linnaeus.

Kingdom-**Animalia:** living things but excluding plants, fungi and some lower forms.

Phylum-**Arthropoda:** segmented bodies with paired jointed legs but lacking the dorsally located central nervous system of the chordates.

Class-**Crustacea:** arthropods with two pair of antennae in front of the mouth. This feature separates crustaceans from insects for our purposes.

Order-**Decapoda:** ten legs.

Families-**Paguridae** and **Diogenidae:** Aquatic hermit crabs, not the major subject of this book.

Coenobitidae: Terrestrial hermit crabs, the major subject of this book.

Genera (of **Coenobitidae**) – *Coenobita:* Consisting of several species of terrestrial hermit crabs; and *Birgus:* just one species, the robber or coconut crab, *Birgus latro.*

A beautiful marine hermit crab, *Calcinus elegans.* Photo by Scott Johnson.

Species of *Coenobita-Coenobita clypeatus;* the only land hermit crab of the tropical and semi-tropical shores of the Western Atlantic.

C. compressus; The land hermit crab of the U.S. Pacific coast.

Other species; Land hermit crabs of the western Pacific and Indian Oceans.

Coenobita clypeatus was first described in 1791 by Herbst, but the specimen was mistakenly labeled "East Indies." Then in 1869 Hilgendorf noted that Herbst's type specimen

The great seaspider crab of Europe can move about on land or in the sea, though it is a sea crab and would die in a few hours if taken out of water. Most crabs are very hardy, and sea crabs can live for days out of water if kept cool and moist. Photo by Gerhard Marcuse.

A weird Australian Barrier reef hermit crab, *Aniculus strigatus*. Photo by Roger Steene.

in the Berlin Museum (which is probably lost by now) was actually a West Indies species that was at that time (1869) called *Coenobita diogenes*, with a small *d*. What happened was that apparently Latreille in 1818 missed Herbst's work and so described the same crab as *Pagarus Diogenes* with a capital *D*. This is not to be confused with *Cancer diogenes*, described by Linnaeus in 1758.

In 1837 H. Milne Edwards reclassified it as *Cenobita Diogenes*. The name was spelled with a capital *D* because it was the name of a person (we don't do that anymore).

Pocock in 1889 took away that capital *D* and then in 1920 Mary Rathbun reclassified it according to the rules of nomenclature, giving Herbst the credit he deserves and im-

The fiddler crab has a large claw which is used for defense and mating. The small claw is for feeding only. Shown is an *Uca* species from Darwin, Australia. Photo by Walter Deas.

FACING PAGE: The upper photo shows a group of soldier crabs on the march. These crabs can run faster than you can. They must have a marine aquarium with a "beach" in order to survive. The lower photo shows a mangrove crab, *Sesarma,* in its burrow in the Seychelles. Photo by Roger Lubbock.

proving the spelling of the genus name, so now we have *Coenobita clypeatus* (Herbst, 1791) the purple-clawed land hermit or soldier crab of the Western Atlantic.

The name *Diogenes* comes up again as a hermit crab in the Pacific and Indian Oceans.

The words *hermit* and *soldier* have been with us for at least two centuries, apparently because the people who named them thought (according to the Rev. Thomas R.R. Stebbing, M.A. in 1893) that they resemble hermits in their cells or warriors in their castles. Well, maybe, and maybe not. There is a bit of West Indies folklore which has it that a military invasion was turned into a rout when at night the troops heard the rumbling of the crabs on their nocturnal scavenging foray. The army thought they were being surrounded and repulsed by a superior force and they left, never to return. Well, maybe, and maybe not.

So, if your terrestrial hermit crab looks like the pictures of it in this book it is most likely *Coenobita clypeatus*. If it was collected on the shores of the Western Atlantic from Palm Beach, Florida south through the West Indies to Venezuela on the northern coast of South America, it is surely this species because there is no other native land hermit crab there.

If your crab came from the U.S. Pacific coast, then it probably is not *C. clypeatus* but it might be *C. compressus,* and if it came from the more western parts of the Pacific or the Indian Ocean it could be any one of a number of similar species, some of which are probably invalid or synonymous with valid forms. The names of a few below were gleaned from various sources dating back to 1893.

Coenobita clupeatus (C. brevimanus): note the spelling of the specific name, cl*u*peatus, not cl*y*peatus. This animal is reportedly an inhabitant of the Moluccas Islands in the Pacific Ocean. I suspect we are looking at a one-hundred-year-old typographical error.

Coenobita rugosus: this species is certainly valid and is

Another fiddler crab of the genus *Uca*. Photo by Marcuse.

found on Aldabra and many other places in the Indian Ocean.

Coenobita perlatus: a beautiful red crab from Australia.

Coenobita clypeatus: this is certainly the wrong name for a living land hermit crab of the Indian Ocean. I mentioned it previously; it keeps cropping up in the old literature. It would take longer to unravel the error than it did to create it.

Coenobita diogenes: also previously noted.

Birgus latro: this is a genuine robber crab and a great climber of tall trees. In its youth it frequently hides its soft parts in a snail or coconut shell, but as it grows it hardens up and by the time it weighs five or six pounds it no longer in-

You can buy almost any type of shell and it will attract your hermit crab if the crab needs a new home. Photo by Dr. Herbert R. Axelrod.

The three shells shown above have just been placed in this position. As soon as they were handled they pulled themselves inside their shells. A minute (exactly!) later, some pulled themselves in even tighter (while some righted themselves and began to crawl away), as shown below. Photos by Dr. Herbert R. Axelrod.

habits a shell of any sort. It has been reported to reach a weight of twenty pounds, but I'm not sure I would put much sincere money on a bet about *that*.

Your crab is likely in a snail shell right now. This might be the fifth or perhaps even the twenty-fifth shell it has resided in since it came out of the sea as a soft-bellied unprotected little crab many years ago. I said it is *likely* in a snail shell. Sometimes hermits are found in shotgun shells, rifle cartridges, light bulb bases, perfume bottles, coconut shells, or fossil snail shells: lacking any other protection for their soft parts, they bury their abdomens in the sand until more suitable accommodations become available.

There is much scientists know about these fascinating animals and still much more we wish we knew. One thing is certain; land hermits do make good household pets. Let us now consider their natural history, their housing and house hunting, their migrations, their appetites (ranging from lettuce to donkeys), their longevity and their sex life.

Fortunately there is not much one *must* know to merely keep a land hermit crab alive, but there is a great mass of interesting information which should help you to enjoy your pet during his long life.

Many crabs have specialized habitats. This crab, *Petrolisthes maculatus,* lives among sea anemones. Photo by Gerhard Marcuse.

This Florida hermit crab, called either "red-legged" or "purple-legged," is *Coenobita clypeatus* and is out-growing its shell. Photo by Dr. Herbert R. Axelrod.

The same *Coenobita clypeatus* as the facing page, front view. Photo by Dr. Herbert R. Axelrod.

Birgus latro, the coconut crab. Photo by Hilmar Hansen.

The Coconut Crab

The famous English pottery maker Josiah Wedgwood had a late-blooming grandson named Charles who was born in 1809 and in 1825 went to Edinburgh (Scotland) to study medicine. However, the young man found he was unfitted and was then directed to theology. He earned a degree in 1831 from Christ College, Cambridge with the idea of becoming a clergyman.

He finally settled for an unpaid job as a naturalist on an English surveying ship destined to circumnavigate the world. This trip of the *Beagle,* December, 1831, to October, 1836, led him to his life's work. Twenty-three years after the trip ended, Charles R. Darwin, Wedgwood's grandson, published his book entitled *On the Origin of Species by Means of Natural Selection, or the Preservation of Favoured Races in the Struggle for Life.*

The first edition of that book consisted of 1250 copies and was sold out on the first day. Over one hundred years later it is still in print, still a best seller. Before embarking on that great classic he spent eight years studying barnacles, and his monographs on these crustaceans are also classics, but less popular.

When Darwin wrote on the natural history of the coral islands of the Pacific, he got into the coconut crab. This is what he had to say:

"I have before alluded to a crab which lives on the cocoa-nuts: it is very common on all parts of the dry land, and grows to a monstrous size; it is closely allied or identical with the *Birgos latro.* The front pair of legs terminate in very strong and heavy pincers, and the last

This lucky hermit crab found a very strong shell and has seal-
ed it up perfectly.

The photographs on the facing page
show a side view of the same shell and
the hermit crab moving about with its
shell. Photos by Dr. Herbert R. Axelrod.

pair are fitted with others weaker and much narrower. It would at first be thought quite impossible for a crab to open a strong cocoa-nut covered with the husk, but Mr. Liesk assures me that he has repeatedly seen this effected. The crab begins by tearing the husk, fibre by fibre, and always from that end under which the three eye-holes are situated; when this is completed, the crab commences hammering with its heavy claws on one of the eye-holes till an opening is made. Then turning round its body, by the aid of its posterior narrow pair of pincers, it extracts the white albuminous substance. I think this is as curious a case of instinct as ever I heard of, and likewise of adaptation in structure between two

Pachygrapsus marmoratus, one of the marine crabs, with her abdomen distended with eggs. This is a rear view of the crab. Photo by Gerhard Marcuse.

objects apparently so remote from each other in the scheme of nature, as a crab and a cocoa-nut tree. The *Birgos* is diurnal in its habits; but every night it is said to pay a visit to the sea, no doubt for the purpose of moistening its branchiae. The young are likewise hatched, and live for some time, on the coast. These crabs inhabit deep burrows, which they hollow out beneath the roots of trees; and where they accumulate surprising quantities of the picked fibres of the cocoa-nut husk, on which they rest as on a bed. The Malays sometimes take advantage of this, and collect the fibrous mass to use as junk. These crabs are very good to eat; moreover, under the tail of the larger ones there is a great mass of fat, which, when melted, sometimes yields as much as a quart bottle full of limpid oil. It has been stated by some authors that the *Birgos* crawls up the cocoa-nut trees for the purpose of stealing the nuts: I very much doubt the possibility of this; but with the Pandanus the task would be very much easier. I was told that on these islands the *Birgos* lives only on the nuts which have fallen to the ground. Captain Moresby informs me that this crab inhabits the Chagos and Seychelle groups, but not the neighbouring Maldiva archipelago. It formerly abounded at Mauritius, but only a few small ones are now found there. In the Pacific, this species, or one with closely allied habits, is said to inhabit a single coral island, north of the Society group. To show the wonderful strength of the front pair of pincers, I may mention, that Captain Moresby confined one in a strong tin-box, which had held biscuits, the lid being secured with wire; but the crab turned down the edges and escaped. In turning down the edges, it actually punched many small holes quite through the tin!"

Incidentally, Charles Darwin's grandfather on his father's side was Erasmus Darwin (1731-1802), also an English scientist, so perhaps Charles came by it naturally.

This crab died within a
few days because its
shell was too small for
its body. It was infected
by mites and began to
desiccate. Photo by Dr.
Herbert R. Axelrod.

This is the same crab
shown on the opposite
page. Here it has
started to weaken and
become unable to bear
the weight of its own
shell. Photo by Dr.
Herbert R. Axelrod.

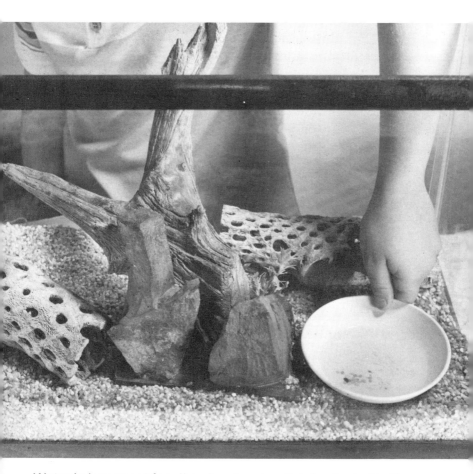

Water is important for all crabs. A water dish implanted in the sand is acceptable, but be sure the crabs can climb out or they might drown! Put sand into the dish to make the crabs feel more at home, or have a stick or rock in the water so they can climb out if they feel it necessary to do so. Photo by Dr. Herbert R. Axelrod.

Other Hermits, Other Land Crabs

Within the class Crustacea, its order Decapoda and the suborder Macrura we find words like sections and tribes and legions and families and genera and species and subspecies and races. Some of these classifications have been wiped out by modern systematists and taxonomists, but I mention a few of the old words here because no one has burned all the old books. Surely, if you dig you will encounter these terms; even if you don't understand them, they can be a clue to animal relationships and to references in texts.

Now, in this decapodan order there is the suborder Macrura with the elongated forms: the hermits, lobsters, crayfishes, prawns and shrimps. Not included in Macrura but in another great suborder, Brachyura, are the typical "true" crabs with ten "working" legs and flattened bodies, 4000 species of fiddlers, rock crabs, spider crabs and that famous edible swimming crab of the U.S. East Coast, the blue crab.

Macrura is much the same as Reptantia in the more modern systems of classifications, but for this book let's simply look at other hermits, other land crabs.

Aquatic hermit crabs have six visible "working" legs and four more for holding and manipulating their shells. In this way they resemble their terrestrial cousins. Of course, their eggs develop under water. Some are scavengers and others eat living plant and animal foods as available. They swap shells. They do well in aquaria. They will die if they are kept out of water for any extended period since their breathing apparatus consists of gills which must be thoroughly wet in

A side view of the same hermit crab as on the facing page.

This hermit crab was bought at a petshop. It is clearly too big for its shell. The pet-shop owner gave the purchaser sound advice in suggesting that he buy some extra shells . . . all larger sizes than the one shown . . . so the hermit crab could exchange shells.
Photos by Dr. Herbert R. Axelrod.

The person in charge of the welfare of the hermit crabs must change the water daily ... or add water more often if necessary. Shallow, rough dishes are fine, providing the crabs can crawl out. Slippery porcelain might be a problem. Photo by Dr. Herbert R. Axelrod.

order to operate. By contrast, land crabs have developed another respiratory apparatus, and some adults will drown if immersed for even as long as one hour. A land hermit crab may enter shallow water in search of a new shell; if it finds the right one with an aquatic hermit in it, the land crab will surely evict or kill the tenant and move into the shell. Cruel, cruel world.

The largest wholly aquatic hermit crab in the Atlantic is *Petrochirus diogenes* (Diogenes again!). This species will inhabit the largest helmet shells *(Cassis)* and the largest conch shells *(Strombus gigas)*. *P. diogenes* is colored solid bright red and its usual home, the conch shell, might be ten inches long.

Smaller aquatic hermits kept as pets include:

Pagurus pollicaris, which grows to five inches and has rough, hairy, broad claws. It is common on the U.S. East Coast.

Pagurus longicarpus never gets larger than three inches and is frequently found on tidemarsh mudflats. This species has relatively long, slender claws and legs and virtually no hairs.

Dardanus megistos, a marine hermit from Australia with hairy red legs. Its two outboard feelers (antennae) are white.

The list of marine hermits you may come upon and keep as aquarium pets is so long that a mere list with brief descriptions would fill a book. Diogenidae has 300 members in its family and the family Paguridae includes at least 300 additional species.

A list of land crabs without shells starts with *Birgus,* the coconut or robber crab, which is mentioned elsewhere in this book.

In the U.S. and throughout the semi-tropical and tropical world are the various species of fiddler crabs, many of which spend much more than half their day out of water. Fiddlers must take a daily dip, but they eat on land and the males display their prowess and their one great fiddle-like claw to

Yes, all of that fits into this small shell! On the facing page is an aquarium which has been set up for fiddler crabs. Photos by Dr. Herbert R. Axelrod.

passers-by on dry or damp land. There are 62 species of fiddlers, worldwide.

Three common U.S. East Coast species are: *Uca pugilator,* the sandy area fiddler, which is often seen in a herd rather than singly.

Uca pugnax, the marsh fiddler. It is a mud burrower and avoids sandy areas.

Uca minax, largest of these three. It is commonly known as the red-jointed fiddler and inhabits the least salty areas of the tidal marsh.

Fiddlers make interesting aquarium pets but must have access to unpolluted brackish water to survive. They are found wherever beaches or marshes face the sea.

One more land crab (out of the multitude) which deserves mention here is the beautiful, gregarious, blue-bodied and white-legged *Mictyris longicarpus. M. longicarpus* ("the long legged one") has two red joints on each of its ten legs. Like *C. clypeatus,* it has been commonly called the soldier crab.

Other land crab names you may come across in pet shops or in the literature are *Ucides, Gecarcinus* and *Ocypode.*

Hermit crabs may be difficult to examine, since they usually pull into their shells when handled. You often can't tell whether they are alive or dead when you buy them. Be sure they have no offensive odor (which indicates they are dead), and be sure you have seen them walk about before they were handled. Photo by Dr. Herbert R. Axelrod.

Choosing a Pet

Pick a specimen of *C. clypeatus* the size you favor and watch it long enough to be sure he has four antennae and at least six legs showing. Two legs will be clawed and the claws will not be the same size: this is as it should be. Actually, your crab is a *decapod* and has ten legs, but four are usually hidden (two are used to hang onto the shell). DO NOT attempt to remove the crab from its shell—most likely its death will result from this treatment. Most hermit crabs would rather die than let go.

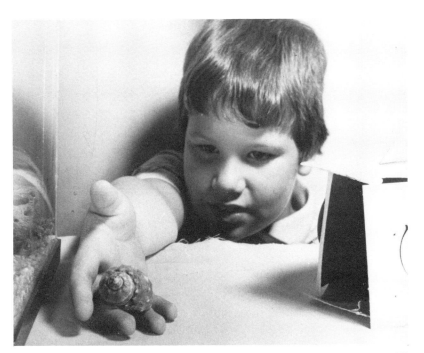

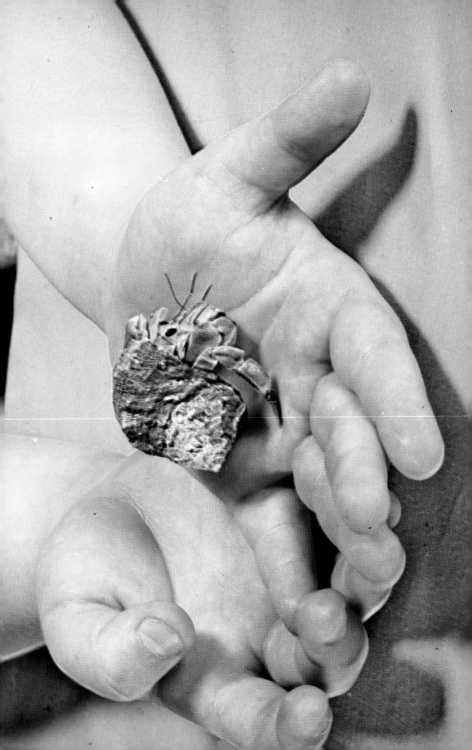

When your hermit crab becomes friendly, he won't hesitate to crawl about on your hands. Take care . . . he sometimes nips you! The photo on the facing page shows how to train him to walk from one hand to the other. Don't drop him. It could kill him. Photos by Dr. Herbert R. Axelrod.

Some crabs are more colorful than others. This is probably a matter of diet and, as noted elsewhere, they are all just one species. The smallest you will probably encounter will hardly be larger than a pea, and the largest might have a really big large claw and inhabit a ten-inch conch shell.

When you get your pet or pets, try to obtain some similarly sized or slightly larger empty shells—your crab will enjoy trying these on and/or swapping from time to time. Since these animals get along together you might want to get a few rather than just one.

At your petshop you might also get an aquarium to house your specimen and a cover to keep cats and rodents from molesting the crab or crabs.

While you are in the petshop you might also purchase a small package of food for your crab. The advantage of this food over what you may provide is that it is known to have all the necessary minerals and nutrients.

Pay no attention to the sex of your crab. It is difficult to determine, and anyway your pet will not reproduce itself in captivity.

The second choice for a pet land hermit crab is the West Coast species, *Coenobita compressus*. It too is interesting and hardy, but unfortunately it tends to be a trifle smelly unless its accommodations are cleaned very frequently.

Shells

Most hermit crabs and all *C. clypeatus* are right-hand twisted so they fit in right-hand twisted snail shells. Fortunately, most snail shells are also right-handed.

Snail shells are from snails which died of causes not related to land hermit crabs—there is no evidence at present to show that the crabs kill snails. The shells may be from aquatic snails or terrestrial or arboreal snails. It is not the source but the fit that counts.

There is no sense listing all the species of snails whose shells fit *C. clypeatus*, but you and your pet can have a ball trying them on for size. There is no reason why a pet crab could not have a dozen shells available in his cage for changing.

In Bermuda there are more large crabs than available large shells from recently deceased snails. This leads to a fascinating report by Fritz Haas of the Chicago Natural History Museum which was published in *Ecology, 31* (1): 152 (1950).Haas refers to our *C. clypeatus* by one of its older names, *Cenobita diogenes*, but that doesn't alter the facts he recounts.

"A very conspicuous inhabitant of all the West Indies, from the Bahamas in the north to Dominica in the south, and of the coast line of North, Central and South America from Key West, Florida to Brazil is a large terrestrial hermit crab which indeed has become so independent of the ocean that it is often seen far away from the beaches and even high up on hills. The name of this rather aberrant crustacean is *Cenobita diogenes*

wardley's
Tree Crab Food

wt.1/2 oz. (14.17 gms

Your petshop has special food for hermit crabs. While scraps will do, the possibility of introducing weed-killers or other pollutants should convince you to buy a tested product. The hermit crab shown below is the trademark of the hermit crab food. Photos courtesy of Kenneth Levey.

The hermit crabs you are most likely to encounter are right-hand twisted. Don't offer them left-hand twisted shells or they won't be able to utilize them. Photo by Dr. Herbert R. Axelrod.

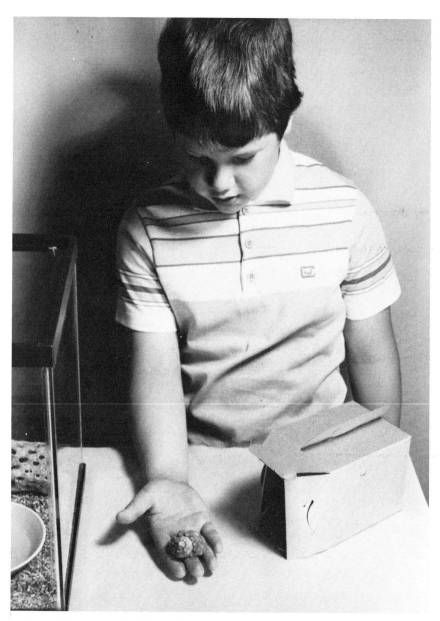

The abdomen of all hermit crabs is soft and needs to be protected by shells of dead snails. Collecting shells is almost as much fun as collecting hermit crabs, so save the shell after the crab outgrows it. Photo by Dr. Herbert R. Axelrod.

Latreille. Like all hermit crabs, this species shelters its soft abdomen in snail shells. In accordance with its stately size, only large snail shells can serve this purpose. In all the localities of its wide distribution, the crab is mostly seen carrying around the heavy, trochoid shell *Livona pica* Linnaeus, which is very abundant throughout that area.

In Bermuda, the aptly named *Cenobita diogenes* is still abundant though at the northern limit of its range. There are no fresh *Livona* shells in Bermuda to serve as hermit crab houses; but fortunately for our hermit, the Pleistocene and even more recently extinct *Livona* left abundant fossil and subfossil shells in the aeolian sandstone deposits that compose the higher ground of the Bermudas. These are excavated by the hermit crab, and used quite in the same way as are the more recent shells elsewhere. Without this supply of large shells, there would not be nearly enough large snail shells for the Cenobitas of Bermuda.

The marine shell *Livona* flourished in Bermuda waters and apparently became extinct there in glacial times. *Cenobita diogenes* also lived on the Bermuda beaches in preglacial times, and used the *Livona* shells to house its soft abdomen then as now. In fact, the abundance of fossil shells in Bermuda sandstone can only be accounted for by the fact that the hermit crabs carried the shells up to all levels while the sands were being blown up and deposited by the winds of the glacial era.

Thus the Cenobitas survived the extinction of their house producer because the activities of their own ancestors had laid up a store of solid shells.

Everywhere in Bermuda one sees the hermit crabs with their *Livona* shells, small and large according to age, in gardens, and on the heath-covered hillsides. There are abundant empty *Livona* shells scattered

Collecting marine hermit crabs, like the one above, can be as interesting as collecting land hermit crabs, but marines require much more care. On the facing page you can see a marine hermit crab trying to make up its mind about a shell change. This is a new twist on the old shell game, I guess!

about, and there can be no doubt that one and the same shell has often served as house for long successions of hermit inhabitants."

In nature *C. clypeatus* will carry the snail shell to protect its soft parts and also to have a source of water to drink and to wet its gills between infrequent rainstorms or its visits to

Before you introduce your hermit crabs to your aquarium, you should be sure they are alive and healthy. Smell them. If they have an offensive odor, discard them in favor of odorless crabs. If you put in empty shells, it is best to drop them into boiling water for a minute or two to be sure they have no parasites in them. Photo by Dr. Herbert R. Axelrod.

freshwater ponds. Furthermore, you may notice that the large claw fits nicely into the opening of the snail shell, effectively plugging it from attack by predators.

You should simply wash out any shells you introduce to your pet's cage to assure that no chemicals remain to irritate the new occupant.

There are several accounts of great shell trading conventions which took place under the eyes of impartial and objective scientific observers. The crabs would congregate on a beach or other open area and for several days thousands of crabs would swap shells and perhaps indulge in a mating ritual. In an article in *Natural History Magazine* dated June, 1945, Arthur Carpenter and Waldo Logan stated that on the Caribean Island called Mona, halfway between Puerto Rico and Santo Domingo, tens of thousands of *C. clypeatus* climbed down off the cliffs and marched to the beaches where they remained congregated for several days, apparently swapping shells and climbing trees (and perhaps engaging in a little lovemaking, too). This is not the only report of this phenomenon, but all are similar and one should suffice.

The following shells are a few of the many that have been known to house *C. clypeatus: Murex* species; crown conch, *Melongena;* whelks; turban, *Turbo;* top shell (West Indian), *Cittarium* (formerly *Livonia)*; star shell; rock shell, *Thais latirus;* moon snail, *Bulbus.*

Hermit crabs are crustaceans and they must shed their hard skin (exoskeleton) as they grow. You've heard of "soft-shell crabs"; well, all crabs are "soft-shelled" from time to time. Photo by Dr. Herbert R. Axelrod.

The facing page shows the hermit crab in its new home. This is a front view of the same shell. Photo by Dr. Herbert R. Axelrod.

Molting

Crustaceans have hard exo-skeletons (shells) and, since they start out in adult form at less than adult size, they must shed their shells from time to time to accommodate this growth. By contrast, a bee has just one shot at how big it will be. As an aside, I here write in the general disclaimer which all zoologists must heed to survive. There is at least one exception to the crustacean molting rule; if you haven't yet thought of it, consider the barnacle.

As hermit crabs grow larger they grow more slowly. A crab the size of a lemon (in its shell) might molt once or twice a year and will probably eat its exo-skeleton shell to get the right mix of minerals (mostly calcium) necessary for its life processes—including making that new shell or perhaps the next one.

Your crab will leave its snail shell and molt its exoskeleton while partially buried in damp saltwater sand, harden up in a couple of days and then search out a larger snail shell to accommodate its new dimensions. So you owe him a new larger shell and perhaps a couple of spares to try on.

One of the hermit crabs owned by Thomas Cuccurullo always croaked and made strange sounds when he was handled, especially when he was restrained from walking. Most of the time he was silent, however. Photo by Dr. Herbert R. Axelrod.

The Voice of the Hermit Crab

Several sounds are emitted from the shelled hermit crabs. The precise sources of these sounds are not established at this writing, but suffice it to say that in addition to the shell rattling, which is always going on among active specimens, they make "croaking-chirping" and "whirring-chirping" and other sounds of a "stridulatory nature."

The sounds are sometimes generated by crabs in the process of fighting over shells. All this was reported by Brian A. Hazlett (1966) in *Ecology*, 47(2), page 316. The article was entitled "Observations on the social behavior of the land hermit crab, *Coenobita clypeatus* (Herbst)."

Your captive pet crab will also make these noises, perhaps for still other reasons, perhaps simply to entertain you.

The best all-around home for your hermit crab is an all-glass aquarium. Your petshop might even have a "leaker" which he'll sell at a discount. The all-glass aquarium has many advantages over other types of hermit crab homes. Photo by Dr. Herbert R. Axelrod.

One of the advantages of a normal aquarium is that lights and protective covers are readily available at moderate prices . . . or, you can make your own from two pieces of glass and some tape. Photo by Dr. Herbert R. Axelrod.

The top of your hermit crab home must be covered. Not only does the cover keep the crabs in . . . but it keeps predatory cats, rats and inquisitive hands out. While the screen cover is acceptable, the glass cover is better, since it holds in moisture and keeps out dust. Photos by Dr. Herbert R. Axelrod.

Migrations

Land hermit crabs are faced with several problems not shared by most other animals. First, they must find empty snail shells of the appropriate size as they continue to grow throughout their long lives. Second, the females must get their eggs to sea water even if they live a mile inland. Third, the male crab must become sexually involved somewhere in these life processes—there is no parthenogenetic reproduction (virgin birth) involved here.

In addition to the shells of dead land and sea snails, an excellent source of empty snail shells for growing hermit crabs is from other growing hermit crabs. A small crab finds an empty oversize shell and moves into it since it is better than what he had. A larger crab in an undersize shell meets that smaller crab in the oversize shell and a trade is accomplished. Sometimes the two crabs don't agree to trade, but the larger one asserts itself and the greater force prevails. On the Dry Tortugas and the Florida Keys and on Hispaniola and on Curacao and on the myriad Leeward Islands and on the romantic Windward Islands also this shell swapping goes on. We know it has been going on for the past few hundred years because there are written records. We suspect that it dates back to eons ago when the first hermit crabs took up living the way they do. There are all kinds of torchlight photographs and magazine feature articles about the long marches and nighttime congregations of shell-swapping crabs. It is also entirely likely that a little mating goes on at this time.

If you get a screen cover that is larger than the aquarium it will be more effective at keeping out insects. Flies sometimes attack hermit crabs and lay eggs in their shells. The maggots may kill the hermit crabs. Photo by Dr. Herbert R. Axelrod.

Adding sand or gravel is one step in setting up the aquarium for hermit crabs. Wash the sand thoroughly in hot water before using it. Remember that the crabs burrow into the sand, so don't make it too deep. About one inch deep is sufficient. Photo by Dr. Herbert R. Axelrod.

Later the females wend their way to the saltwater shore where they hang onto mangrove roots and drop their eggs into the water or they stand at the water's edge and literally throw their eggs out into the briny deep. No, I didn't think this up—these reports, by objective observers in recognized scientific journals of these nighttime gatherings, are a matter of record.

For *C. clypeatus* most assemblies take place in August and September for shell swapping and, most likely, mating. Later the females with their clusters of eggs wend their way to salt water with no male company, help or encouragement.

Reproduction

There is a lot we don't know, but the few facts which have been nailed down certainly suggest that still more effort is justified. It seems that when the ancestors of the land hermits left the sea, they didn't quite leave it entirely. The adult still returns for a dip or a drink from time to time and the eggs will not develop except in seawater.

To begin at the mating, this is accomplished on land and apparently the female need not recently have molted (as is the case with aquatic crabs) in order to copulate.

The eggs are subsequently extruded onto the outer surface of her abdomen, where they hang like a cluster of tiny grapes until she kicks them off onto the ocean water. The eggs hatch promptly and the young crabs (called zoea) grow and metamorphose until after four to six zoeal stages they begin to more nearly resemble their parents. This metamorphic stage is called the glaucothoe. Now you can easily recognize claws, and the eyes are mounted on eyestalks. In this form they work their way back to land, slowly first in shallow sea water and then on damp beaches and edges of brackish or freshwater ponds. They find tiny snail shells and then for the first time we recognize them as typical soft-bellied hermit crabs.

Female crabs the size of the first joint of your thumb and in their second year are capable of reproduction, but the number of eggs they produce is far smaller (about 1000) than what you might expect from an adult the size of one's fist (about 40,000 or 50,000). Obviously most of the zoea don't make it. If they did, the Antilles would be buried in land hermit crabs.

Sometimes old shells have been around too long, and the inhabitants outgrow them. If no other shells are available they have to stay in them, but constant dragging of the shell over sharp gravel wears the shell thin. The same shell (in better condition) is shown on the facing page. Photos by Dr. Herbert R. Axelrod.

Female land hermits prefer to stay out of the deep water and are known to kick or throw their ripe eggs into the water from a dry perch seemingly whenever they can accomplish this. They really make an effort to avoid entering the water to release their eggs, yet they know that without seawater the eggs will not hatch. Intelligence? Instinct?

Size

Specimens of *C. clypeatus* weighing a pound are considered to be full-sized, but this calculation is not "naked weight." The shell might represent more than one half of this total weight.

Robber (coconut) crabs have weighed in at six pounds and are reputed in one book to reach twenty.

Care and Cages

Feed your pet as much as it will eat. Remove uneaten food as it spoils. Provide fresh clean water in a shallow container which is easy for a crab to enter and leave. Avoid slippery bottoms and tippy or deep bowls. Your crab might actually drown if it cannot get out of its water dish.

Provide warmth and sunlight but also provide shade and cool places in the cage or aquarium. Remember that the angle of sun varies with the hour and with the season. Your crab will be more active at night, but that is not to say he is a nocturnal creature.

The ideal temperature range is the same as that of Key West, Florida or the island of Curacao, say 71° to 93° Fahrenheit (22° to 34° Centigrade). The air should not be damp all the time and the ground or sand or gravel should be generally dry on the surface but damp as one digs into it.

The cage or aquarium bottom should be covered with an inch or more of crushed coral, coral rock, crushed clam and oyster shells or limestone. Crabs on a pure silica sand substrate don't do as well as those that have access to lime. The cage should also have a piece of wood, perhaps a branch of driftwood, for the crabs to crawl on or climb, but remember that they are agile and curious and prone to escape. Be sure that the distance from the tip of the highest point they can climb to the top of the cage is more than twice the height of the crabs. Remember that they can form bridges by climbing on each other's "backs." If you should cover the cage (the ideal cage is an aquarium), the cover should be fastened or weighted to prevent escapes.

Hermit crabs need warmth and sunshine. The sand should be dry on top but moist underneath so they can dig down to hide or cool off. Photo by Dr. Herbert R. Axelrod.

Keep the sand flat and put a piece of wood or rock for them to climb on. Be careful that the crabs cannot escape by climbing on top of one another to reach the exit which you *thought* was impossible for them to slip through!

69

Old bird cages make excellent homes for hermit crabs, but they become too cold in the winter in northern climates, and they tend to rust and become unsightly.

A stainless steel birdcage is a good land hermit crab cage, but you should bear in mind that the bars must be spaced for the crab and not for the shell which the crab happens to be carrying around. A crab may well leave his shell to effect an escape.

The substrate should be deep enough to be moist at the bottom, because your crab may prefer to moisten its breathing apparatus in damp sand rather than in a dish of water. Also, when land hermits molt they leave their shells and bury themselves in moist sand until the new shell hardens on the legs and thorax. Ideally a hermit crab should be able to completely bury itself in damp sand. Screen cages of relatively inexpensive ½"-square galvanized mesh are great because your crab will get a lot of good mileage from going up, down and around his universe with claws and legs fitting nicely in the squares.

Don't waste good money on a new birdcage for your pet unless it is all stainless steel, because the salt water he will enjoy dipping in from time to time will eventually work its way to the metal parts of the cage and that will be the end of it.

Ideally the cage or aquarium should have: live plants, places to climb, clean fresh water and clean ocean water made by mixing sea salt with tapwater to achieve 30 or 35 parts per thousand by weight. A quart of water is about a

If you can't get an all-glass aquarium, get one with a stainless steel frame. These are mostly obsolete nowadays, but there are some still to be found. They are equally as effective as the all-glass tanks except for their cement, which might contain a poison for the crabs. Coat the cement with silicone cement (available from your petshop).

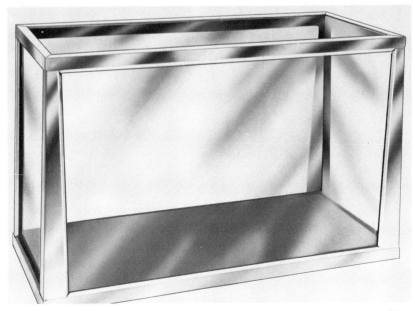

Do not use a piece of driftwood which extends over the top of the aquarium. Your hermit crab will climb up the branch and escape. Escapes usually end up with a crab that is either eaten by a small animal or stepped on by a larger one! Photo by Dr. Herbert R. Axelrod.

Cactus skeletons are excellent for your hermit aquarium. They provide lots of toeholds for the crabs and, being hollow, they are utilized for refuges. More than one crab will use the same log in which to hide. Photo by Dr. Herbert R. Axelrod.

scant liter or 1000 cubic centimeters or 1000 grams of water. An ounce of salt weighs about 29 grams. So *very roughly* an ounce of salt in a quart of water will approximate seawater salinity. Your friendly postmaster or delicatessen proprietor will help you weigh out a few one-ounce portions of salt, I'm sure. Especially if you say it's for your pet crabs; then he will understand.

There are not many diseases you can cure or control except by proper nutrition and hygiene. Lost legs will be regenerated eventually. Undersized shells should be exchanged for larger ones to accommodate growth. Damaged shells should be replaced promptly for protection of soft parts from both parasites and dehydration.

This is an ideal setup for your hermit crabs (or turtles . . . or both). The light is used to see and to keep the hermit crabs warm during cold nights. The dish in the corner is too slippery for the crabs, but it is filled with stones which enable the crabs to crawl out. Photo by the author.

An excellent way to heat the hermit aquarium is to put a heater in a Bell Mason jar. Thermostatically controlled heaters used for aquariums are available from your local petshop. Set the thermostat so that a temperature of around 75°F. is maintained.

There are some parasitic or possibly commensal mites which will attach themselves to your pets, and these are hard to control. The chemical which will sureley kill an arthropod parasitic mite will also kill an arthropod crustacean decapod hermit crab. If you discover your crab is infested with mites, you might pick them off with tweezers. To accomplish this, you must first get your pet out of its shell. Not easy. You might drill a tiny hole in the second or third whorl of the crab's snail shell or you might accomplish this task by application of heat at the same place—try a soldering iron. There is no great hurry. Use your God-Given-Intelligence and Take-Your-Time. There is no reason for the famous "The operation was a success—but the patient died."

A complete hermit crab setup needs constant housecleaning. Uneaten food should be removed every few days and replaced with fresh food. The water must be checked daily. The dish must never run dry. Photo by Dr. Herbert R. Axelrod.

New additions to the hermit crab aquarium are usually carried home in a small box ... though a paper bag will do just as well. Keep your eye on new crabs to be sure they are healthy.

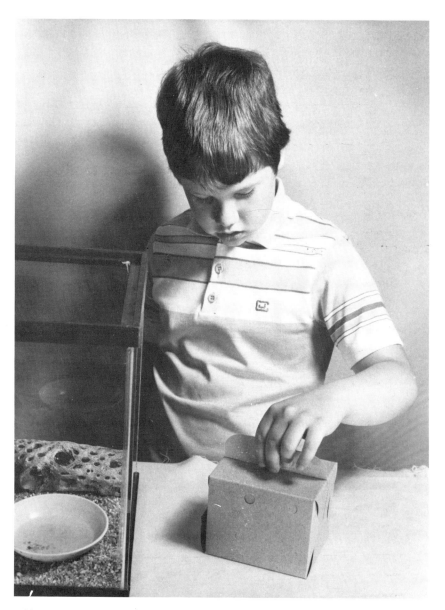

Keep the small cardboard box in which the hermit crabs may have come. It is handy for holding your crabs while you're cleaning their tank, or for taking back to the petshop for exchanges. Photo by Dr. Herbert R. Axelrod.

In 1928, A.S. Pearse described and named a mite which is specifically a parasite on *Coenobita clypeatus* (then still known as *C. diogenes*). He named it in honor of Dr. H.E. Ewing, and his paper was published in 1929 as "Two new mites from the gills of land crabs" in the *Papers of the Tortugas Laboratory, Carnegie Institute, Washington, 26:* 227-230.

The mites are less than one millimeter long—about 1/25 of an inch.

C. compressus (and perhaps *C. clypeatus* also) has been parasitized by a botfly which places its eggs on the soft abdomen of the crab. These maggots then burrow in and the crab's death results. This is an unusual situation and should not trouble you.

An ideal setup for hermit crabs which worked for years for the
model, Thomas Arthur Cuccurullo. The dish (see lower
photograph) was a favorite hiding place for the crabs; they all
burrowed around and under the dish, since they liked the
splashing dampness as the crabs entered and left the dish.

Hermit crabs make nice pets, and you should handle them as much as possible. They soon learn not to bite, but don't give them the chance to catch your finger when they are frightened. Photo by Dr. Herbert R. Axelrod.

Food

Your pet crab will eat from time to time. If conditions of light, heat and moisture are right he will eat heartily. If not, he will not. What will he eat? Anything from a lettuce leaf to a dead donkey is fair game.

Lettuce was fed to a land hermit for 11 years at the Smithsonian Institution in Washington. But the crab never reached more than half the normal adult size. (Chace, *Crustaceana*, 1972.) In *Studies on the Fauna of Curacao and Other Caribbean Islands*, "On the Ecology of *Coenobita clypeatus* in Curacao," *44* (76): 1-138 by P.A.W.J. de Wilde, 1973, it was reported that a dead donkey provided food for weeks to hundreds of hermit crabs. The crabs also fed in refuse dumps, kitchen gutters, etc., even coming to coffee grounds.

In *The Crab and its Relatives* by Phillip Street (1966, Faber and Faber Limited, London, p. 133) it is stated that this crab, "which lives in Florida, is credited with eating the young of terns and other ground-nesting birds."

Fresh mangrove leaves, bananas, avocados, lettuce and coconut meat—also the entire husk and shell of coconuts—also peanut butter and bread—also young terns that had not yet learned to fly. All this on page 279 of *Sea Frontiers, 10*(5), 1964, by William M. Stephens.

If your hobby carries you from the land hermit crab to the robber or coconut crab *Birgus latro* the scope of the diet extends according to Captain J.Y. Cousteau, who, in *The Living Sea*, wrote that a coconut crab stowed away and in a

5,000 mile trip ate 6 champagne crates—but couldn't open the bottles to wash them down.

Odor plays an important part in the crabs' search for food. They are attracted to decaying meat more readily than to fresh meat. They also aim at roasted coconut meat, coffee grounds and ripe fruit like bananas and apples. Mangrove leaves and *Pandanus* fruit are eaten, and so also is mangrove sap.

Your petshop can provide you with a prepared basic diet for your crab. This will assure you that all the necessary minerals are available for growth and the manufacture of new exo-skeletons. You may also supplement this prepared food with a bit of donkey from time to time.

There is no "perfect" home for hermit crabs. They need fresh water, food, and a place to climb and hide; fresh plants also are helpful, so stuff some greens between the rocks. A tight-fitting screen cover keeps in the crabs, but the joints of the cover might allow flies and small insects to crawl in, so an over-sized cover might have some advantages. Photo by Dr. Herbert R. Axelrod.

A top view, looking down into a nicely set up terrarium. (The one on the facing page, actually.)

Almost every Caribbean island, including the Florida Keys, has thousands of hermit crabs. You can find them, usually hiding during the day, by turning over fallen branches of the coconut palms. At night they are easily spotted with a strong light. But don't take them. Read the chapter on "conservation" first.

Conservation

Visitors to the Miami area and the Florida Keys encounter land hermit crabs if they poke around under the dead fronds of palms during daylight hours or if they walk on beaches or in woods near beaches at night. The crabs are easy to catch and interesting and easy to transport and many do end up as captive pets. Now, everyone knows and many well-meaning people are quick to point out that each female hermit crab produces from 1,000 to 50,000 eggs per year and since she only has to reproduce herself and her mate the remainder will never be missed. The fallacy in the argument is simply that she and her mate are *adults*. They exist today because 1,000 to 50,000 eggs per year were deposited five or ten years previously.

If each collector who visited Florida took home one microscopic waterborne hermit crab zoeal larva—or even 100—they would never be missed. But let's look at it another way—you can collect a thousand acorns a day 'till the cows come home and the environmental impact will still be too small to measure, but try cutting down a thousand oak trees per day and see what happens. Same with hermit crabs.

Worse yet, the environment is getting progressively more hostile for these creatures. People build seawalls and separate the sea bench from the woods. Insecticides and herbicides are lethal to crabs as well. Draining tidemarshes or filling them also effectively wipes out crab populations since this transition area is where the young crab emerging from the sea makes its adjustment to living on land.

There is no question but that *C. clypeatus* is less common in many places than it had been. Legislation has been pro-

A hermit crab eating a piece of dry biscuit. Biscuits are the
usual fare for crabs, but they don't live too long on this diet.
Your petshop will have regular hermit crab food.

A healthy hermit crab with its hinged antennae! Photo by Dr. Herbert R. Axelrod.

posed to restrict the capture, sale or ownership of these interesting animals. It is unlikely that any such law will be easy to enforce if it is ever enacted.

There are tremendous numbers of land hermit crabs, all of the same species, throughout the entire area between southern Florida and northern Venezuela. They are not endangered, that is obvious. The pet industry will hardly make a dent in the total population of these crabs, but a concerted collecting effort on one beach in Miami or on one Key in the Florida Keys or on one island in the Caribbean Sea could easily wipe out a local population or reduce it to a size which might impair shell-swapping or congregational mating since these activities could actually be triggered by a critical minimum number of individuals. Who knows, maybe that was the true fate of the passenger pigeon.

For those of us who do not become moralistic or otherwise don't extend our ethical thinking to include arthropods, the question of protection for land hermit crabs still deserves some attention. For one thing, they are great scavengers and will convert useless dead animal and plant tissues into useful alive animal tissue. In various parts of the world they are an important bait used by fishermen. They are edible. A quart of high quality oil may be obtained from a single large coconut crab. They transport land and water snail shells to remote places to confound future palaeontologists. They make interesting stridulating and whirring noises to break the stillness of the tropical night. They repel invading armies. They make fine pets.

Longevity

The best evidence I can find in print for longevity of *C. clypeatus* is the note by Fenner Chace, Jr., which was mentioned in the chapter on food. It remained about the same size for eleven years and we can assume that to get to its captive size took an additional two years, at least. Were it not for the disease that killed it (fungus infection), I suspect it could have easily gone on another eleven years with no trouble.

When a shell has been used over and over again by generations of hermit crabs, it becomes worn and loses a lot of its color and beauty. In nature this has the advantage of making it less obvious, thus safer from predators. Photo by Dr. Herbert R. Axelrod.

The same shell as the facing page shows the colorful hermit crab snuggly fitted into its shell! Photo by Dr. Herbert R. Axelrod.

References

This short selection was derived from an extensive bibliography created by Dr. Patsy A. McLaughlin, Florida International University, Miami, Tamiami Campus.

Bliss, D.E., 1968. Transition from water to land in decapod crustaceans. *Am. Zool., 8:* 355-392.

Borradaile, L.A., 1903. Land crustaceans. In J.S. Gardiner (ed.), *The fauna and geography of the Maldive and Laccadive Archipelagoes.* Cambridge, The University Press, 1: 64-100.

——————, 1910. On the land and amphibious Decapoda of Aldabra. *Trans. Linn. Soc., London,* 2, 13(3): 405-409.

Carpenter, A. and W.H. Logan, 1945. Hermits don't always live alone. *Natural History, New York, 54,* (6): 286-287.

Catesby, M., 1771. *The natural history of Carolina, Florida, and the Bahama Islands.* London, published by author. *2* (1743).

Chace, F.A., Jr., 1972. Longevity of the West Indian terrestrial hermit crab *Coenobita clypeatus* (Herbst, 1791) (Decapoda, Anomura). *Crustaceana, 22* (3): 320.

——————— and H.H. Hobbs, Jr., 1969. Bredin-Archbold-Smithsonian Biological Survey of Dominica. The freshwater and terrestrial decapod crustaceans of the West Indies with special reference to Dominica. *Bull. U.S. Nat. Mus.,* 292: 1-258.

Gruber, A. and J.B. Shoup, 1969. Crabs move ashore. *Sea Frontiers, 15:* 364-375.

Haas, F., 1950. Hermit crabs in fossil snail shells in Bermuda. *Ecology, 31* (1): 152.

Hazlett, B.A., 1966. Observations on the social behavior of the land hermit crab, *Coenobita clypeatus* (Herbst)., *Ecology*, 47 (2): 316-317.

Iverson, E.S. and R.H. Skinner, 1977. *Land hermit crabs in nature and as pets*. Miami, Windward Publishing Inc., 32 pp.

Pearse, A.S., 1929a. Observations on certain littoral and terrestrial animals at Tortugas, Florida, with special reference to migrations from and to terrestrial habitats. *Papers Tortugas Lab., Carnegie Inst., Washington, 26:* 205-225.

_____, 1929b. Two new mites from the gills of land crabs. *Papers Tortugas Lab., Carnegie Inst., Washington, 26:* 227-230.

_____, 1932. Observation on the parasites and commensals found associated with crustaceans and fishes at Dry Tortugas, Florida. *Papers Tortugas Lab., Carnegie Inst., Washington, 28:* 103-115.

Provenzano, A.J., Jr., 1962. The larval development of the tropical land hermit *Coenobita clypeatus* (Herbst) in the laboratory. *Crustaceana, 4*(3): 207-228.

Radinovsky, S. and A. Henderson, 1974. The shell game. *Natural History, New York, 83* (10): 23-29.

Stebbing, T.R.R., 1893. *A history of Crustacea, Recent Malacostraca*. International Scientific series. London, Kegan Paul, Trench, Trubner & Co. Ltd., 466 pp.

Stephens, W.M., 1964. Hermit crabs. *Sea Frontiers, 10* (5): 272-284.

Street, Phillip, 1966. *The crab and its relatives*. Faber and Faber, London.

Wilde, P.A.W. de, 1973. On the ecology of *Coenobita clypeatus* in Curacao, with reference to reproduction, water economy and osmoregulation in terrestiral hermit crabs. *Studies on the fauna of Curacao and other Caribbean Islands. 44* (76): 1-138.

Hermit crabs have minimal requirements, but their needs must be served. Give them warmth, water, the proper food and cleanliness, plus new homes (shells) when necessary and the crabs could live more than ten years. Photo by Dr. Herbert R. Axelrod.